ALTERNATIVE ANTHEM

T0272778

John Agard was born in Guyana and came to Britain in 1977. His many books include six collections from Bloodaxe, *From the Devil's Pulpit* (1997), *Weblines* (2000), *We Brits* (2006), *Alternative Anthem: Selected Poems* (2009), *Clever Backbone* (2009) and *Travel Light Travel Dark* (2013). He was awarded the Queen's Gold Medal for Poetry 2012.

He won the Casa de las Américas Prize in 1982 for *Man to Pan*, a Paul Hamlyn Award in 1997, and a Cholmondeley Award in 2004. *We Brits* was shortlisted for the 2007 Decibel Writer of the Year Award, and he has won the Guyana Prize twice, first for *From the Devil's Pulpit* and then for *Weblines*.

As a touring speaker with the Commonwealth Institute, he visited nearly 2000 schools promoting Caribbean culture and poetry, and has performed on television and around the world. In 1993 he became the first Writer in Residence at London's South Bank Centre, which published *A Stone's Throw from Embankment*, a collection written during that residency. In 1998 he was writer-in-residence for the BBC with the Windrush project, and *Bard at the Beeb*, a selection of poems written during that residency, was published by BBC Learning Support. He was writer in residence at the National Maritime Museum in Greenwich in 2007.

He is a popular children's writer whose titles include *Get Back Pimple* (Viking), *Laughter is an Egg* (Puffin), *Grandfather's Old Bruk-a-down Car* (Red Fox), *I Din Do Nuttin* (Red Fox), *Points of View with Professor Peekaboo* (Bodley Head) and *We Animals Would Like a Word with You* (Bodley Head), which won a Smarties Award. *Einstein, The Girl Who Hated Maths*, a collection inspired by mathematics, and *Hello H₂O*, a collection inspired by science, were published by Hodder Children's Books and illustrated by Satoshi Kitamura. Frances Lincoln Children's Books published his recent titles *The Young Inferno* (2008), his retelling of Dante, also illustrated by Satoshi Kitamura, which won the CLPE Poetry Award 2009, and *Goldilocks on CCTV* (2011). His anthology *Hello New* (Orchard Books, 2000) was chosen by the Poetry Society as its Children's Poetry Bookshelf Best Anthology.

He lives with the poet Grace Nichols and family in Sussex; they received the CLPE Poetry Award 2003 for their children's anthology *Under the Moon and Over the Sea* (Walker Books).

John Agard
ALTERNATIVE ANTHEM

SELECTED POEMS
WITH *JOHN AGARD LIVE!* DVD

BLOODAXE BOOKS

Poems copyright © John Agard 2009
Film copyright © Pamela Robertson-Pearce 2009
Music copyright © Keith Waithe 2009

ISBN: 978 1 85224 823 9

First published 2009 by
Bloodaxe Books Ltd,
Eastburn,
South Park,
Hexham,
Northumberland NE46 1BS.

Second impression 2015

www.bloodaxebooks.com
For further information about Bloodaxe titles
please visit our website or write to
the above address for a catalogue.

Supported by
ARTS COUNCIL
ENGLAND

LEGAL NOTICE
All rights reserved. No part of this book may be
reproduced, stored in a retrieval system, or
transmitted in any form, or by any means, electronic,
mechanical, photocopying, recording or otherwise,
without prior written permission from Bloodaxe Books Ltd.
Requests to publish work from this book
must be sent to Bloodaxe Books Ltd.
John Agard has asserted his right under
Section 77 of the Copyright, Designs and Patents Act 1988
to be identified as the author of this work.

Cover design: Neil Astley & Pamela Robertson-Pearce.

Printed in Great Britain by
Bell & Bain Limited, Glasgow, Scotland.

For my mother Anna DeSouza

ACKNOWLEDGEMENTS

This edition includes poems selected from John Agard's collections *Man to Pan* (Ediciones Casa de las Américas, 1982) and *Limbo Dancer in Dark Glasses* (Greenheart, 1983), reprinted with *Come Down Nansi* (2000) in *Weblines* (Bloodaxe Books, 2000); *Mangoes and Bullets* (Pluto Press, 1985; Serpent's Tail, 1990) and *Lovelines for a Goat-Born Lady* (Serpent's Tail, 1990); *From the Devil's Pulpit* (Bloodaxe Books, 1997); *Half-Caste* (Hodder Children's Books, 2004); *We Brits* (Bloodaxe Books, 2006); and three collections illustrated by Satoshi Kitamura, *We Animals Would Like a Word with You* (Red Fox, 1996), *Hello H$_2$O* (Hodder Children's Books, 2003) and *Einstein, the Girl Who Hated Maths* (Hodder Children's Books, 2003).

'Toussaint L'Ouverture Acknowledges Wordsworth's Sonnet "To Toussaint L'Ouverture"' first appeared in *'Earth has not any thing to shew more fair': a bicentenary celebration of Wordsworth's sonnet 'Composed upon Westminster Bridge, 3 Sept. 1802*, edited by Peter Oswald, Alice Oswald and Robert Woof (Shakespeare's Globe and The Wordsworth Trust, 2002).

'Dialogue' was commissioned by the English-speaking Union and read at Westminster Abbey for the ESU's 85th anniversary on 26 June 2003, thanks to Valerie Mitchell.

'Windrush Child' was first performed on *Blue Peter* and appeared in *Bard at the Beeb* during a residency at the BBC in 1998 to mark the 50th anniversary of the arrival in Britain of the *Empire Windrush*.

'On a Yazoo Stem' first appeared in *The POT Anthology* (New Departures, 2005), edited by Michael Horovitz.

'A Hand on a Forehead' was commissioned by the Barbican Education Department, thanks to Gillian Barker, in response to Sebastião Salgado's exhibition 'Migrations: Humanity in transition' held at the Barbican Gallery.

The live performances on the DVD were at Soho Theatre, London, on 10 October 2007 (with thanks to Geraldine Collinge and Russell Thompson of Apples & Snakes) and at Havant Arts Centre, Hampshire, on 22 October 2008 (with thanks to Amanda O'Reilly and Simon Grey). Special thanks are due to Pamela Robertson-Pearce for her film, and to Keith Waithe for his musical contribution to the Havant set (www.keithwaithe.com).

Thanks to Satoshi Kitamura for the cover and to Paul Taylor for the photo.

CONTENTS

1

poems from

MANGOES AND BULLETS
&
WE BRITS

Talking to Plants

Always talk to your plants.
Sit back and watch them flourish.
Good advice. Of course we presume
that all plants speak English.

Speak slowly, watch them bloom.
If necessary shout each syllable.
Their little ears are ready vessels
for a shower of the Queen's vowels.

Never mind if it's a China rose
or an African violet.
Better yet, recite a bit of English Lit.
See abundance spring at your fingertip.

So I spoke like an Oxford don
to my wilting rhododendron.
It wilted more. As for my drooping shrub,
my words only seem to draw more slugs.

O plants, what is it that makes you grow?
I watch my immigrant neighbour's patio
with a sense of distant envy.
Tell me, plants, must I address you in Punjabi?

Heart Transplant

No puff
no pant
check out
a heart transplant

let's swop
your heart
for mine
heart transplant
the new life line

come on baby do the heart transplant
come on baby do the heart transplant

experiment number 1
put the heart of a bird
into a stone

the stone sings
the stone grows wings
wondrous flight
of a common thing

experiment number 2
a medical breakthru
put the heart of your average politician
into a common stone

stones grow paranoid
stones grow suspicious of grass
stones hurl themselves into the void

alas
will stones develop a paunch
seeking the votes of God

Finders Keepers

This morning on the way to Charing Cross
I found a stiff upper lip
lying there on the train seat

Finders Keepers
I was tempted to scream

But something about that stiff upper lip
left me speechless

It looked so abandoned so unloved
like a frozen glove
nobody bothers to pick up

I could not bear to hand in
that stiff upper lip
to the Lost & Found

So I made a place for it
in the lining of my coat pocket

and I said
Come with me to the Third World

You go thaw off

Forever Afters

Served, as always, for the last.
The tail end of the menu.
The main course's epitaph.
A pudding knows the meaning
of waiting one's turn in queue.
Patience is what puddings know best.
And when all face the final test
on that day of reckoning,
puddings will array their glory
down to the smallest gooseberry,
for every pudding knows one truth –
that the first shall be last
and the last shall be first.
Yes, puddings shall have the last laugh
when the sweet inherits the tooth.

Listen Mr Oxford don

Me not no Oxford don
me a simple immigrant
from Clapham Common
I didn't graduate
I immigrate

But listen Mr Oxford don
I'm a man on de run
and a man on de run
is a dangerous one

I ent have no gun
I ent have no knife
but mugging de Queen's English
is the story of my life

I dont need no axe
to split/ up yu syntax
I dont need no hammer
to mash/ up yu grammar

I warning you Mr Oxford don
I'm a wanted man
and a wanted man
is a dangerous one

Dem accuse me of assault
on de Oxford dictionary/
imagine a concise peaceful man like me/
dem want me serve time
for inciting rhyme to riot
but I tekking it quiet
down here in Clapham Common

I'm not a violent man Mr Oxford don
I only armed wit mih human breath
but human breath
is a dangerous weapon

So mek dem send one big word after me
I ent serving no jail sentence
I slashing suffix in self-defence
I bashing future wit present tense
and if necessary

I making de Queen's English accessory/to my offence

Reporting from the Frontline of the Great Dictionary Disaster

Why has the English dictionary grown so thin?
Why is it weeping between its covers?
Because today is the day
all words of foreign origin
return to their native borders.
Linguists are rioting in the streets.
Crossword lovers are on hunger strike.
But words are voting with their feet
and familiar objects across the British Isles
have staged a mass evacuation.

Anoraks
have been seen flying off backs
remaking their Innuit tracks.

Bananas
hands forming a queue
are now bound for a Bantu rendezvous.

Hammocks
leave bodies in mid-swing
and billow back to a Carib beginning.

Pyjamas
without regard to size or age
take off on a Hindu pilgrimage.

Sofas
huddle themselves into caravans,
their destination – the Arabian sands.

Even Baguettes
(as we speak) grab the chance
to jump the channel for the south of France.

This is a tragedy
turning into a comedy
for reports are reaching us by satellite
that in the wee hours of the night
the ghosts of ancient Greeks and Romans
have been preparing an epic knees-up
to mark the homecoming of their word-hoard.
Stay tuned for live and direct coverage
on this day a dictionary mourns its language.

What More Can One Ask of Cricket?

To bridge continents with glorious uncertainty.
To leave a legacy of unpredictability.

Mixed Marriages

Mixed marriages do have their advantages.
We express our needs and tiffs in two languages.

Moorish

The more the Morris Dancers strut their knees
And flash their swords, the more the Moors are pleased.

Shakespeare Addresses Tabloids After Dark Lady Rumour

She was my dark secret, O that dark lady
whose hairs of wires sparked more than a sonnet.
Let the paparazzi probe her mystery.
How decipher night's hidden alphabet?

Let's say she was a lass unparallel'd
but I'm no kind of cur to kiss and tell.
And journalists know nought who know not this:
to be unnamed is a nameless bliss.

I'll not let on, no I'll not let on.
Let's say she was my Nile on Avon,
my badge of ebony in an ivory world,
my breathing gateway to the womb's word.

Fie on you who would have me expose her!
Let her be anon, and again anon.

By the Light of Fruits

Beside

the strawberries'
red gleam

the plums'
purple glow

the granny smiths'
green sheen

I spied
with my little eye

the bananas
in transition –

their half-yellow
glimmer

their half-ripe fingers
clenched in slowly

ripening
revelation –

a sunny salutation
from one horizon

to another.

English Girl Eats Her First Mango

If I did tell she
hold this gold
of sundizzy
tonguelicking juicy
mouthwater flow
ripe with love
from the tropics

she woulda tell me
trust you to be
mellowdramatic

so I just say
taste this mango

and I watch she hold
the smooth cheeks
of the mango
blushing yellow
and a glow
rush to she own cheeks

and she ask me
what do I do now
just bite into it?

and I was tempted
to tell she
why not be a devil
and eat of the skin
of original sin

but she woulda tell me
trust you to be
mysterious

so I just say
it's up to you
if you want to peel it

and I watch she feel it
as something precious

then she smile and say
looks delicious

and I tell she
don't waste sweet words

when sweetness
in you hand

just bite it man
peel it with the teeth
that God give you

or better yet
do like me mother
used to do

and squeeze
till the flesh
turn syrup
nibble a hole
then suck the gold
like bubby
in child mouth
squeeze and tease out
every drop of spice

sounds nice
me friend tell me

and I remind she
that this ain't
apple core
so don't forget
the seed
suck that too
the sweetest part
the juice does run
down to you heart

man if you see
the English rose
she face was bliss
down to the pink
of she toes

and when she finish
she smile
and turn to me

lend me your hanky
my fingers
are all sticky
with mango juice

and I had to tell she
what hanky
you talking bout

you don't know
when you eat mango
you hanky
is you tongue

man just lick
you finger
you call that
culture
lick you finger
you call that
culture

unless you prefer
to call it
colonisation
in reverse

Palm Tree King

Because I come from the West Indies
certain people in England seem to think
I is a expert on palm trees

So not wanting to sever dis link
with me native roots (know what ah mean?)
or to disappoint dese culture vulture
I does smile cool as seabreeze

and say to dem
which specimen
you interested in
cause you talking
to the right man
I is palm tree king
I know palm tree history
like de palm o me hand
In fact me navel string
bury under a palm tree

If you think de queen could wave
you ain't see nothing yet
till you see the Roystonea Regia
– that is the royal palm –
with she crown of leaves
waving calm-calm
over the blue Caribbean carpet
nearly 100 feet of royal highness

But let we get down to business
Tell me what you want to know
How tall a palm tree does grow?
What is the biggest coconut I ever see?
What is the average length of the leaf?

Don't expect me to be brief
cause palm tree history
is a long-long story

Anyway why you so interested
in length and circumference?
That kind of talk so ordinary
That don't touch the essence
of palm tree mystery
That is no challenge
to a palm tree historian like me

If you insist on statistics
why you don't pose a question
with some mathematical profundity?

Ask me something more tricky
like if a American tourist with a camera
take 9 minutes to climb a coconut tree
how long a English tourist without a camera
would take to climb the same coconut tree?

That is problem pardner
Now ah coming harder

If 6 straw hat
and half a dozen bikini
multiply by the same number of coconut tree
equal one postcard
how many square miles of straw hat
you need to make a tourist industry?

Find the solution
and you got a revolution

But before you say anything
let I palm tree king
give you dis warning
Ah want de answer in metric
it kind of rhyme with tropic
Besides it sound more exotic

Encounter

What makes you you
and me me?

What makes us us
and them them?

Is it the anthem
that rouses to attention?

Is it the flag
we wave on occasion?

Is it the passport
that punctuates a border?

Is it the unofficial
stamp of undeclared genes?

Is it the voice's colour
that's a dead giveaway?

Or is it the baggage
of skin and creed

that makes one say
not one of us, one of them?

And so missing the chance
of getting closer

to that image
reflected in the mirror –

yourself unmasked
in the Other's plumage.

Toussaint L'Ouverture Acknowledges
Wordsworth's Sonnet 'To Toussaint L'Ouverture'

I have never walked on Westminster Bridge
or had a close-up view of daffodils.
My childhood's roots are the Haitian hills
where runaway slaves made a freedom pledge
and scarlet poincianas flaunt their scent.
I have never walked on Westminster Bridge
or speak, like you, with Cumbrian accent.
My tongue bridges Europe to Dahomey.
Yet how sweet is the smell of liberty
when human beings share a common garment.
So, thanks brother, for your sonnet's tribute.
May it resound when the Thames' text stays mute.
And what better ground than a city's bridge
for my unchained ghost to trumpet love's decree.

...Thou has left behind
Powers that will work for thee; air, earth, and skies;
There's not a breathing of the common wind
That will forget thee; thou has great allies;
Thy friends are exultations, agonies,
And love, and man's unconquerable mind.

– from Wordsworth's sonnet to Toussaint L'Ouverture,
a former slave, who led a revolution that would lay the
foundation for Haiti to become the first Black republic (1804).

The Ascent of John Edmonstone

(The freed black slave who taught Darwin
taxidermy at Edinburgh – 1826.)

My name rings no bell
in the ears of science
but footnotes know me well –

footnotes where history
shows its true colours
and passing reference is flesh

for I am John Edmonstone,
whose name is little known
to evolution's white ladder.

But Darwin will remember me,
just say the black man who taught him
Egypt's ancient art of taxidermy.

To think that we should meet
in Edinburgh of all places
few doors apart on Lothian Road.

No mention then of savage races.
In those days we were two bird-stuffers
mounting mortality in feathers.

We were each other's missing link
colleagues upright on the chain of being
a pair of wingless apes condemned to think.

Newton's Amazing Grace

*(John Newton [1725-1807], slave ship captain, who converted to
the ministry and composed many hymns, including 'Amazing Grace'.)*

Grace is not a word for which I had much use.
And I skippered ships that did more than bruise
the face of the Atlantic. I carved my name
in human cargo without a thought of shame.
But the sea's big enough for a man to lose
his conscience, if not his puny neck.
In the sea's eye, who is this upstart speck
that calls himself a maker of history?
It took a storm to save the dumb wretch in me.
On a night the winds weighed heavy as my sins,
I spared a thought for those poor souls below deck.
Terror made rough waters my Damascus road.
Amazing grace began to lead me home.
Lord, let my soul's scum be measured by a hymn.

Memo to Professor Enoch Powell

In the name of Alpha and Omega
I address you, Professor Enoch Powell.
Shall I forward this to heaven or to hell?
What's immigration like in the afterlife?

Did St Peter hassle you at the pearly gates?
Or Satan question your right to immigrate?
Say you have nothing to declare but your dust
and your ghost may yet gain refugee status.

It must be a supernatural culture shock,
even for a classical scholar,
to meet angels in turbans and haloes of dreadlocks
carousing along eternity's corridors.

And clovenfoot men in bowler hats
waving their tridents like union jacks.
But since you yourself were not averse to verse,
where paradox blesses and purity is a curse,

I'll quote, Professor, from your own words:
'The flocks of migrant birds,
They are all poems...' But alas
your view of migration could only embrace

those feathered immigrants of space –
an example of what happens, Professor,
when the intellect's shining mirror
is cracked by a terror of the Other.

But as translator of the New Testament,
Paradise may yet grant you some reprieve.
Then again with the classics up your sleeve,
Dante's *Inferno* may prove your element.

Here, on earth, it's nearly spring.
February shimmers with rivers of blood
that still flow in the veins of black and white.
And migrant poems bloom in inner-city light.

Jet-lagged Prophets

When Jesus landed at Gatwick
his style was far from three-piece slick.
So they sniffer-dogged his hippy hair
and sandalled feet in need of washing.

When Buddha showed up at Heathrow
he was taken in for questioning.
He said he had nothing to declare
but his passport had a suspicious glow.

When Mohammed made it to Dover
they thought to themselves: asylum seeker,
though his papers were in order
and Dover not his idea of Mecca.

O jet-lagged prophets who come in peace,
what made you think it legal to be meek?
Your restless feet will know no resting ground,
when even prayers are frisked for a weapon.

Gandhi's Revenge

Those Brit tastebuds are in for a morale boost.
Chicken tikka massala is home to roost.

Alternative Anthem

Put the kettle on
Put the kettle on
It is the British answer
to Armageddon.

Never mind taxes rise
Never mind trains are late
One thing you can be sure of
and that's the kettle, mate.

It's not whether you lose
It's not whether you win
It's whether or not
you've plugged the kettle in.

May the kettle ever hiss
May the kettle ever steam
It is the engine
that drives our nation's dream.

Long live the kettle
that rules over us
May it be limescale free
and may it never rust.

Sing it on the beaches
Sing it from the housetops
The sun may set on empire
but the kettle never stops.

2

poems from
COME DOWN NANSI

Who gave word? Who gave word? Who gave word?
Who gave word to hearing?
For Hearing to have told Anansi
For Anansi to have told the Creator
For Creator to have made the Things?

TWI PRAISE SONG FOR SPIDER

Flesh to Fancy

1

Nansi
Anansi
Ananse
Anancy
Nancy

however spell me
merely invoke me

and from my web-bed
I will rise

the eightlegged one
will take on twolegged guise

will answer to the name
of uncle or aunty

and give flesh to fancy

The Coin of Birth

Spinning mama squatted her hairy horizon
on a bed of atoms

and out of the gushing purse of her wombspace
I came screaming with the coin of birth

and midwife moon threw back her head
in recognition of the long-awaited one

spider's word incarnate on whose tongue
stories shall be twinkling currency

the one with the never-ending navel string
tying continents in umbilical knots

and as if to mark the marvel of my birth
I Nansi closed one mint-eye for mischief sake

my eight legs tapping epics from the cosmic floor

Anancy's Thoughts on Colours

(for Andrew Salkey)

Long-time back in the beginning beginning
when sky-god Nyame was handing out colour,
sky-god Nyame take one look at me Anancy
and say pick whichever colour you fancy.

I cast me eye high
I cast me eye low
I work up me brain to studify
dis colour issue,
spare it a thought or two.

Red stare at me from deep gash of skin
Yellow try to tempt me with sunflower grin
Green wink at me with brazen leaf-eye
White beckon me with subtle shift of cloud.
And all dis time blue so damn calm and proud
as if one shimmer and Anancy done blue.

I work up me brain good-good.
I turn to sky-god Nyame.
I say sky-god Nyame, I done ponder
dis thing you call colour issue.
Thank you but no thank you.

Let Snake, Tiger, Parrot and dem
hustle up for colour hand-out.
I will stay original dark
as it was in the beginning beginning,
spinning web of bright imagining,
cherishing the gift of cunning.

How Ananse's Waist Suffered
a Double-Dine Dilemma

My waist wasn't always this thin.
Let me take you back to the beginning

when plump waist pillowed Spider's side.
Oh yes, I was quite a different size.

It all happened, if I'm honest,
because of my little food weakness

for all roads lead to the pot,
and I always say first come gets it hot.

So when news cordially reached me
of plans for big knees-up feed-up spree

in north town and south town, yes, all two,
I cogitated what to do,

for even with these eight legs of mine
I can't be in two places same time.

If I go north town feast, my mouth
will miss out on south town feed-out.

If I go south town wine-and-dine,
north town partake will pass me by.

So I devised a strategema
to deal with this double-dine dilemma.

Tying two long ropes round my waist
I said to my first son, make haste

take the end of this rope, go north town.
When feasting start, pull hard, I will come.

Then I summoned my second son
and gave him similar instructions:

Take the end of this rope, go south town.
When feasting start, pull hard, I will come.

With my two ropes and two sons
covering the feasts from both directions

The plan was to stay still and wait
for signal to sweet-mouth celebrate

How was I to know that both north and south
would simultaneously start sharing out?

Well, to cut a long story short,
those obedient boys pulled hard from south and north

you'd swear it was tug-o-war tussle
while I paid the price with my middle

which I'm pleased to say
lives on in legend and riddle.

How Tiger Played Dead and How Anansi Played Along

One day Tiger hale and hearty,
stripes resplendent, body well fed.
Next day, Tiger take so poorly,
his wife say Tiger gone and dead.

Well, this news didn't ring too right,
at least not to my Anansi ears.
Tiger seemed free from mental cares
and showed no sign of failing might.

Wariness of mind may be my fault
but such tidings must be pinched with salt.
For while death comes on horseback, it's true,
Tiger can't dead just so out the blue.

Caution persuaded me to suspect
Tiger was staging his own death.
But I kept my thoughts to myself
and observed the turn of events.

Sure thing, Tiger and his madam
had jointly concocted up a plan
to have their hungry-belly way
with the small creatures of the land.

For when these came to mourn and pay
last farewell on that sad day,
Tiger planned to spring up from deceased
and play the true devouring beast.

The Tigers grinned and pre-set
their table for a funeral feast.
And Mrs Tiger lived up to her role,
putting on her best widow's mourn:

Tiger dead! My husband dead, Aye-o!
Here today, gone tomorrow
O life has dealt a cruel blow.
Welcome friends, share my sorrow.

Donkey, Dog, Goat, Pig, Parrot –
that whole inquisitive lot –
had gathered to commiserate.
Tiger meanwhile lying in state.

I sort of grieved on the sidelines
and decided to play my trump card.
I drew Tiger's grieving wife aside
and offered my condoled regards.

To all intents, you're a widow.
I take my hat off to your sorrow.
And no disrespect to your broken heart
but tell me truly, did Tiger fart?

So you come to mock, not pity me?
I am surprised at you, Anansi.
I assured her on the contrary,
for I had travelled widely

And no tiger really breathes its last
without a rite-of-passage fart.
Only after that final blast
can a dying tiger depart.

My words of course reached Tiger's ear
for I had spoken fortissimo,
and comforting the weeping widow,
I said Mrs Tiger have no fear

If your husband is yet to pass wind,
then he is still in the land of the living.
And Tiger unable to hold back
exploded from his bottom-crack.

A farting corpse, needless to say,
sent all creatures scurrying away.
Don't thank me, I said. Thank the wind.
And returned pronto to my ceiling.

The Embodiment

since spider feel at home
with thread and rope

I thought I'd try Eu-rope
(the name sounded promising)

so I headed for England
land of hope and unfinished glory
like Schubert's symphony

leaving Amsterdam to Surinam spinners
and Paris to Martinique weavers

arrived at Heathrow not quite light
eight nothing-to-declare suitcases
balanced on eight metropolis-dreaming legs

soon got used to juggling eight cups of tea
like I was spider embodiment of Earl Grey

and nobody made any comment
till I metamorphosed into proper
tophat ascot gent

and bought a piece
of property in Kent

then the pauses
became pregnant

and I heard myself say

No I'm not on holiday
Spider is here to stay

My Brollie

My grey suit matching English skies
I took a spiral stride
down the April pavements.

I had made a truce with rain
and almost felt Anglo-saxon.
My at-homeness was heaven-sent.

A bobby doffed his helmet
in my foot-weaving direction
and the pigeons kept their distance.

All the signs told me to dance
or at least open my brollie
like some forgotten icon

So whether clouds play foul or fair
I wave my brollie's royal web
and embrace the anonymous air.

How Nansi Got Lead Part in Swan Lake

Face-masked, nerves unwracked, stomach butterfly-free,
at audition time I presented my eightlegged mime
and white leotards swanleapt in spotlight

Soft as fufu I glided in the tutu that covered my cucu,
doing a pas–de–deux me one twice times over, true-true,
and pirou-eighted to make old spider grandmother proud.

They all agreed I was born for upstage swan part.

On first night I received standing ovation of flowers
followed by coronation of rave reviews.
To be honest, it was just a regular ruse.

But papers hailed my artistry as spellbinding.
First time ballet buffs had ever witnessed
ballerina swan transformed to spider gracefully unwinding.

Anancy's Thoughts on Hospitality

Let heart
be a hut
thatched with love

open to visitors
from below
and above

and when the stranger
calls to your door

even if there's no
room on your heart-floor
to spread
a sleeping mat

remember to say
(just in case)
say to the thin-waist
traveller who's leaving

Come back, friend,
you're welcome
to a corner
of my ceiling

and even
the fly
in my pot.

Nansi Airobics

Spin and weave
bend those knees

spiral torso
low as limbo

tangle limbs
in webs of vertigo

the dance ends
when your thread runs out

Anancy's Thoughts on Couples

Teeth and tongue must bite
when they share one mouth-roof.

Two buttocks must brush
when they share the same bed.

New cloth comes from the rub
of spindle and thread.

Apply the law of the loom
to warp and weft of bedroom.

How Aunty Nansi Singularly Widened
the Debate on Plural Identity

What a high-brow-knitting controversy
when Aunty Nansi on topical TV show
presented herself as proof of plurality.

Dressed in a side-splitting sari
a red gold and green necklace for Selassie
and snazzy tartan shawl for the cold

Aunty Nansi sat up to her full height
face straight to camera in front row
her stockings laddering the limelight

And with fingers nail-polished lilywhite
same as she'd womanicured her every toe
she gesticulated to gentleman host:

'Now Mr Kilroy, you tell me
Am I Afro-Celto-Euro-Indo
or just beautiful byproduct of cosmos?'

And with her question spiralling like a ghost
Aunty Nansi took the opportunity
to wave hello to her folks across the galaxy.

Thirteen Ways of Looking at the Old Tie

A striped reminder
of the embers of empire.

*

A nostalgic neck-binder
for a post-colonial evening.

*

An emblem that divides
insiders from outsiders.

*

A prop for suicide
by way of strangulation.

*

An icon of Eton
worn even with the heat on.

*

A signifying signpost
to the nearest pubic station.

*

A crested spearhead
into male bonding.

*

A formal demarcator
of respect for the dead.

*

A diagonal entry
into the Royal Artillery.

*

A cross-sexual accessory
of gender-bending politics.

*

A Freudian substitute
for the umbilical cord.

*

A subliminal throwback
to the Neanderthal club.

*

In Nansi's motley wardrobe
the tie, on the other hand,

could be quite simply
a polka dot silk paddle

to row the sea of circumstance.

3

poems from
MAN TO PAN

When Columbus set out to sail around the sphere, he set in motion a series of migrations/vibrations bringing all the cultures of the world to the Caribbean. Trinidad became a crucible in which a unique mix of creolisation gave birth to pan. This son of the trinity, born out of the labour throes of slavery and colonialism, now reverberates around the globe in the opposite direction, striking a healing chord of reconciliation back to Europe and the East, s/panning both hemispheres.

CY GRANT, Ring of Steel *(pan sound and symbol)*

I can visualise pan back on the street
The only paradise jumping to the beat
I can see pan beating everywhere
From the Savannah to Independence Square
My prediction is as usual
Pan will be back for Carnival.

LORD KITCHENER, More Pan *(calypso)*

Pan Recipe

First rape a people
simmer for centuries

bring memories to boil
foil voice of drum

add pinch of pain
to rain of rage

stifle drum again
then mix strains of blood

over slow fire
watch fever grow

till energy burst
with rhythm thirst

cut bamboo and cure
whip well like hell

stir sound from dustbin
pound handful biscuit tin

cover down in shanty town
and leave mixture alone

when ready will explode

*

On new ground we scatter old drum seeds
letting them shape a destiny of sound
unburdening the iron in our blood.
Thunder roots new voice in steel
and lightning seams metal with song.

Who would have dreamed that Shango heart
would beat this far would follow us
across strange water to stranger earth
rising to thunder from oildrum rust?

*

DELIVER
hammer
blow
on steel/
DELIVER
steel
belly
groan/
DELIVER
steel
skin
stretch/
DELIVER
steel
flesh
shudder/
DELIVER
steel
womb
pulse
& burn/
DELIVER
till
birth
cry
of steel
mudder
say
PAN
bornNN
PraisSSEE GoddDD

*

Let each hammer blow
shaping
concave womb
of old oildrum
be the voice
of Shango
thunder

Let each lick of fire
tempering
blue-hot metal
be the splintered tongue
of Shango
lightning

Let this sweet kiss of fever
Let this blackness of mirror
Let this websong of spider

to panman's
shaman
touch surrender
surrender

*

is the sinking
    of metal
is the cleaving
    of a feeling
is the weaving
    of a dream
is the sounding
    of a scream
is the drumming
    of a heart
is the grounding
    of a hurt
is the pounding
    of a rage
is the wounding
    of a night
is the grooving
    of blackness
is the moving
    of a man
      of
    PAN

for the taste of fire
to the thrust of chisel
in a web of sound
in old oildrum
to a beat of steel
to tones of blood
to tunes of love
by slash of stars
by trickles of light
to the embrace

*

Rivulets of melody
spread out
like lines of destiny
spread out
from me palm
of flesh
to you palm
of steel

Man to pan
ah feel
we grow as one
from root to sky
ah feel
we flow as one
when blood meet iron
in one suncry

*

Beat it out man
beat out the hurt
beat it out
to riddum of steel/
feel
panblood flow
watch the dream
grow
from things unshaped
to real/
beat it out man
beat it out
beat out the rape
of the whip
shadow
the burn and blow
on gaping skin/
beat it out man
beat it out
beat out the weight
of history
scar/and/hate
beat it out man
beat it out
beat out the bleed
And spill
of seed
to waste/
beat it out man
beat it out
beat out
a new message
from de middle/
passage
womb of riddle/
beat it out man
beat it out
beat out the burden
of history
sound
beat it/heal it/shape it
confound
wounds
with vision

*

Steelpan
dark web
of Anancy

black pool
of ancient
memory

help break
this chain
of history

help beat out
this pain
in yuh sweet womb

mek me
born again

*

When you hear
dem silksmooth notes
spiralling
from steelweb
and feel
dem raindrop threads
of sound
weaving riddum to blood
you know
is not for nothing
they call it
spiderpan

*

Reflections
of black
moons
tuned
to filaments
of sound
fragment/disperse/entwine
in a web
of harmonies
reflections
of drumbeat
chainsweat
knifeedge
memories
reflections
in dark
poolface
of pan
disturbing
       the gaze
          of centuries

4

poems from
LIMBO DANCER IN DARK GLASSES

The limbo dance becomes the human gateway which dislocates (and therefore begins to free itself from) a uniform chain of miles across the Atlantic.

WILSON HARRIS: 'History, Fable and Myth'

limbo
limbo like me

sun coming up
and the drummers are praising me

out of the dark
and the dumb gods are raising me

KAMAU BRATHWAITE: 'Islands'

Rainbow

When you see
de rainbow
you know
God know
wha he doing –
one big smile
across the sky –
I tell you
God got style
the man got style

When you see
raincloud pass
and de rainbow
make a show
I tell you
is God doing
limbo
the man doing
limbo

But sometimes
you know
when I see
de rainbow
so full of glow
& curving
like she bearing child
I does want know
if God
ain't a woman

If that is so
the woman got style
man she got style

Limbo Dancer's Soundpoem

Go
down
low
     low
        low

show
dem
what
you know
        know
           know

let
limb
flow
     flow
          flow

as sound
of drum
grow
     grow
         grow

& body
bend
like bow
      bow
         bow
            limb/bow
                low
                  low
                    low
                      limb/bow

Limbo Dancer's Mantra

LIMB/BOW

Pronounce dem
two syllable
real slow
you hear me
real slow

LIMB/BOW

Savour dem
two syllable
till glow
spread from head
to tip of toe

LIMB/BOW

Contemplate dem
two syllable
in vertigo
of drum tempo

LIMBO

Meditate on dem
two syllable
calm as zero
vibrate to sound
let mind go

& forget the stick
I tell you
don't think about the stick

that will take care of itself

Once

Once they gave a smile
& called me ethnic

once they looked amazed
& called me kinetic

once they applauded
& called me magic

now they say get out from under there
we know you're hiding under that stick
come out now or we'll shoot you hear

Limbo Dancer's Reading Habits

Limbo dancer reads the *Wretched of the Earth*
bending over backwards

Limbo dancer reads *How Europe Underdeveloped Africa*
bending over backwards

Limbo dancer reads Che Guevara's diary
bending over backwards

Limbo dancer reads Angela Davis' autobiography
bending over backwards

Limbo dancer reads *Capitalism & Slavery*
bending over backwards
& has chained every word to memory

But limbo dancer also reads the *Kama Sutra*
bending over backwards
as well as *The Joys of Natural Childbirth*

Some believe this is what makes limbo dancer
capable of sustaining multiple revolutions

Limbo Dancer at Immigration

It was always the same
at every border/at every frontier/
at every port/at every airport/
                              of every metropolis

The same hassle
from authorities

the same battle
with bureaucrats

a bunch of official cats
ready to scratch

looking limbo dancer up & down
scrutinising passport with a frown

COUNTRY OF ORIGIN: SLAVESHIP

Never heard of that one
the authorities sniggered

Suppose you got here on a banana boat
the authorities sniggered

More likely a spaceship
the authorities sniggered

Slaveship/spaceship/Pan Am/British Airways/Air France
It's all the same
smiled limbo dancer

Now don't give us any of your lip
the authorities sniggered

ANY IDENTIFYING MARKS?

And when limbo dancer showed them sparks
of vision in eyes that held rivers
                              it meant nothing to them

And when limbo dancer held up hands
that told a tale of nails
                    it meant nothing to them

And when limbo dancer offered a neck
that bore the brunt of countless lynchings
                    it meant nothing to them

And when limbo dancer revealed ankles
bruised with the memory of chains
                    it meant nothing to them

So limbo dancer bent over backwards
                    & danced
                    & danced
                    & danced

until from every limb
flowed a trail of red

& what the authorities thought
was a trail of blood

was only spilt duty-free wine

so limbo dancer smiled
saying I have nothing to declare
& to the sound of drum disappeared

The Reason

Because they know
I have centuries of bending behind me

because they know
I can bend so low
barbed wire cannot hold me

they felt a concentration camp
would not be safe enough for me
& though 6 million Jews did not agree

they decided to send me to Chile
& there they held me facedown in a stadium

I thought they would have smashed my knees
as they did Victor Jara's hands
instead they simply called me missing

But because they know
I have centuries of bending behind me

they felt a stadium
would not hold me for very long

so they transferred me to Southern Africa
where I was placed in solitary confinement
but it was the same in that other continent

I thought they would have manacled my ankles
as they had done with Biko

But because they know
centuries ago
I had learnt to live with manacles

they decided to banish me
to a living hell
& the name of Mandela rang a bell

But because they were told
they had got the wrong man/or the wrong woman

since to them my sex was indecipherable
& in any case unimportant

& knowing I was capable of a million disguises

they gave the order to shoot on sight
without question
anything seen bending backwards

so if you should see anywhere
a rifle aimed towards the rainbow

you must know
I limbo dancer

am the reason

5

poems from
FROM THE DEVIL'S PULPIT

God is good and the Devil isn't bad either.

IRISH PROVERB

One man's god was his enemy's devil.

BARBARA G. WALKER:
The Women's Encyclopedia of Myths and Secrets

The Devil is as much a manifestation
of the religious sense as are the gods.

JEFFREY BURTON RUSSELL: *The Devil*

In no other religion is there anything comparable in
power and fearful monstrosity to the Christian Devil.

KAREN ARMSTRONG: *The Gospel according to Woman*

The Devil, it seems, has a million and one disguises.

PETER STANFORD: *The Devil: A Biography*

The Devil will take your soul and keep it.
I will take your sole and heel it.

SIGN AT DUBLIN SHOEMENDER'S

Spell my name backwards.
Ask yourself: Have you LIVED?

Yours truly, THE DEVIL

Applecalypse

I

Eva, mind if I call you Eva?
Have you got something against fruit?
Come on Eva speak the truth.

Have you truly experienced
the absolute yum of plum
the afterglow of avocado
the summery of strawberry
the fleshly figment of fig?

Don't tell me you're allergic
to the mythic munch of pomegranate
the oracular pulp of orange
the glandular grapple
with a simple apple.

A veritable juice downpour
in the valley of the throat.
And if I may misquote:
'An apple a day keeps the devil away.'

II

If all that apple spiel
doesn't make you feel
to tongue steal
and unpeel
the little orb
shining as anything
from the harvest
of Hesperides

If all that apple hype
doesn't make you a ripe
target for marketing –
a prime sampler
of the puckered product –
and it won't cost a buck
today you're in luck
Then answer me truly –
when again will you get this chance
to combine Vitamin C
with a thirst for ecstasy?

III

Such a difficult customer, this Eva.
I wonder what makes her waver –
so irresistible, when irresolute,
I for one would certainly crave her
if I were dissolute.
But she knows me better than anyone.
She's already seen through my snakesuit.

My God, she's testing my powers to ad lib.
All right Eva, I take what you say
about this business of the rib:
that the whole thing was rigged.
Of course it was your arching bone
– nothing to do with the Most High throne –
and with a little help from a hissing word,
that launched Adam on his way
from that nondescript bed of clay.
Now he's off naming, blissful as a bird.
Sometimes I get the urge to rib him.
But we'll keep that our little secret.

Anyway, back to the business of fruit.
Let's get down to taking temptation by the root.

> Come on Eva.
> Try a half.
> Between us
> we could write
> an epitaph
> to the forbidden.

> Bite.

IV

And after she had bitten
her face was burdened
with a glow most sweet

And all that first man
back from a bout of naming
could say was 'Helpmeet

There'll be trouble from above.'
For he who had given names
to creeping thing and flying form

Had stumbled on no word for Love.

V

And even as his teeth were sunk into the apple globe
he felt for a split second at the crossroads.
Part of him succoured by the unnamed juice
Part of him fearing the sword of Justice.

Well Adam, boy, allow me to say
you've come a long way from anonymous clay.
Knowledge is beginning to open its door.
So bite on. Explore the cavern of the core.

But expect some retribution from the Big Chief
That Sovereign of the straight and narrow path.
So I'll be as brief as the famous fig leaf
that will adorn the altar of your private parts.

Helpmeet. Is that all you could call your better half?
She who weaned you to the wisdom of the grass
and succumbed to the secrets of the stars.
Adam, believe me, Eva knows where it's at.

Never mind that flaming advocate of wrath
Who will call your rapture insolence.
What's Eden after all but a den of innocence.
Remember, nothing ventured, nothing gained.

Think of all the sunlight and the rain
that goes into the grooming of a single apple.
If my argument seems serpentine and subtle
How accept the pleasure without the pain

Turn your back on Eden for the endlessly possible
See temptation as bounteous benediction.
As for original sin? A clear misnomer.
A chincanery of words. A sleight of tongue.

That stirring of limb for limb and skin for skin
Is not exactly what I would call sin.
That ancient urge to bridge the solitary abyss.
Come on you two. Go for it. The first kiss.

VI

And so the mouth held forth its promise
like a baboon's pleasurable pouch noticed
for the first time, signalling another path
crooked and wide as temptation,
shedding in a split second its innocent tongue
for one only the gospel of flesh could fathom.

And he whose mouth was given to naming
was suddenly silenced by the un-utterable
And she to whom apocalypse was apple
trusted in the testament of the moment
since eternity was void of sound and scent.
Thus the tongue exalted in its own oracle.

And how I hissed to the beat of Revelation
and gloried in the frailty of right and wrong.

VII

The first unrecorded kiss.
Then Eden thrust its pelvis
in the face of you know who.

And who'll blame those original two
for wanting to try out their tongue
when a noun was a beautiful bliss.

So I'll tread with them
the cobble stones of temptation.
But I'll lift their feet towards the horizon

even as they stumbled, my frail ones.

VIII

Only the serpent in the dust
Wriggling and crawling,
Grinned an evil grin and thrust
His tongue out with its fork.
CHRISTINA ROSSETTI: *Eve*

No, Christina, I did not grin an evil grin.
In fact I wished them luck in their new enterprise
pleased with myself for having opened their eyes
to the limitations of Paradise.

No one in their right mind would suggest
that this pair had just commited original sin
so wondrous the sun shone
in the sanctuary of their skin
and what was done could not be undone.
If you looked keenly you'd detect a certain glow
as if guilt had wrapped them in its subtle bloom.
But there was no room for regret
or ruminations on the pros and cons of sin.

Adam had a sheepish schoolboy sort of grin
as if he had braved the headmaster's cane
and secretly would do the same again.
Besides, he could always pass the blame
and say she talked him into it.
But my God, how he'd miss assembling
those animals and giving each a name.
If they could counsel him now, would fowl and beast
pity his mortal trembling?

Eva meanwhile picked a myrtle sprig
and made it into the first ribbon
So Eden lingered in her hair.
And in the final moment of their parting
she thought she saw the serpent raise
the formidable flower of his eye
and she knew that look
would be companion to her solitary days
like a perfumed petal pressed between a book.

Reservation for Two

I

Waiter, bring me a bottle
of your best Baudelairean wine
(opened with the Devil's corkscrew).
Tonight I feel like a vintage swine.

II

Book me a room with a view
in the London Hilton.
I'm having a naughty weekend
with the shadow Minister Milton.

III

Reserve a table for two
in your most nookie corner.
I'm in the mood for five-star food
and talk enlightening and lewd.

IV

Serenade me with harps and horns
and a sonata by Tartini.
Tell the candle at both ends
to burn O so slowly.

On First Name Terms

Hey. None of this Beelzebub business.
Lighten up. No more Prince of Darkness
and all that Devil's Advocate
kind of stuff. I'm your mate.
It's all right to call me Dev
and I'll call you Les or Mags or Trev.
Formality stinks. Don't say evil. Say Ev.

Lucifer the Perfect Host

I

Whom did you expect to answer the doorbell?
A horned host in flaming robes of hell?

My cigarette holder is my only trident
and cloven feet were never my bent.

II

It's good to be entertained by moonlight
when the angel of darkness puts on her tights

and offers you a bowl of forbidden fruit.
That's how she separates the boy from the brute.

III

Please accept my apology, dear guest,
If I'm not the fiend you were led to expect.

Make yourself at home and do as you wish.
I'll put on my mask and bring out the swish.

IV

Do let me take your coat and your conscience.
I will hang them both by the entrance.

Sorry about my directions. I did say
bear right till you come to the brimstone driveway.

V

Vegetarian? Then avoid the goat stew.
But may I tempt you with a brew

of my special bifurcated root with cheese
I picked up duty-free in Hades.

VI

O, the one in the hat, she's Tiamat. Stunning.
And the good fellow beside her is Robin.

Now that we've all been introduced,
why not mingle, hang loose, be seduced.

House-Warming

Open your heart
and I will give you
the key to hell.
No need to knock
or ring the bell.
Just let yourself in.
Make yourself at home
like a toad
under a rock.
A wart on a skin.

Ars Conversationis

The Devil is an excellent conversationalist
who speaks in parenthesis –
who scatters the spoor of commas
where pauses may or may not matter –
who breaks the bread of repartee
to grace a situation's gravity –
who drops the occasional remark
that dispels the listener into the dark
where all contradictions unite –
But being a good listener, well informed, polite,
the Devil will never put you on the spot
by asking *Have you seen the light or not?*

Of Course the Devil Speaks Latin

Membrum genitale
Pudendum muliebre
Fellatio in flagrante
Cunnilingus uninterruptus
O conjugation unctuous
if you'll excuse my latin.

In Keeping with R.S.V.P. Protocol, the Devil Cordially Responds to a Costume Party Invite

Shall I come as a he?
Shall I come as a she?
How shall I bedeck me?
O decisions decisions.

Shall I come with feathered wing
of a fallen celestial?
Or shall I slip into something
a little more bestial?

Maybe my Goat-labelled number,
designed when horns were all the rage?
Or shall I wear my Ass's mask
complete with rampant appendage?

Maybe a skirt of serpent skin
set off with forked accessory?
Or shall I don the livery
of a lying attorney?

Shall I come costumed
as God's articulate Ape?
Or shall I assume
a more teasing shape?

A G-stringed angel aglow
with a bulbous halo?
Or shall I strut my Siren dress
to lure you to the naked test?

Shall I drape the robe of Vicar
above my ordained knickers?
Or shall I act the Buffoon
in a protuberant pantaloon?

How do I make up my mind
when one's wardrobe flaunts such a line
of motley pedigree?
Ah, the life of a V.I.P.

But since my presence will be missed,
I'll simply come as The Other,
so when the party's fully pissed
I'll play the Scapegoat, brother,

for all the insults that you hiss.

A Light Traveller

The Devil always travels light
and never suffers from jet lag.
A toothbrush like a small trident
in an overnight bag.
A copy of Dostoyevsky
for a little light reading.
A change of underwear.
Nothing unnecessary.
Nothing, as they say, to declare
except a duty-free conscience
and a passport that never expires.

By Their Fruits You Shall Know Them

What fruit did Hitler eat? Or Stalin?
Or we ourselves who used that murderous
miracle at Hiroshima.
ARCHIBALD MacLEISH

See, an ordinary man reaching toward a bowl.
Even his moustache anticipates the aroma
of an apricot, a peach, or I daresay, an apple.

No subtle serpent lies hidden in its core.
Only fragrant fruit in simple porcelain
adorning his mother's dining-table.

So let psychiatrists unearth some childhood trauma
or some perversion of the brain to explain
the forked path of murder or miracle.

I've said it before and I'll say it again:
Each heart sows the seeds of its own Satan.
This simple truth makes it possible

for a man to shine an apple on his sleeve
while contemplating the extinction of millions.

Colour of Evil

What is the colour of evil I asked of Yellow
who led me past Wordsworth's daffodils and Van Gogh's sunflowers
till we came to flashbacks of Vietnam
where the sun's rays were yellow robes of mourning.

What is the colour of evil I asked of Green
who showed me the springtime hills that held a child's scream
and the grass lost its innocence
to the god of forensic evidence.

What is the colour of evil I asked of Brown
who spoke of the romance of autumn leaves
but I saw baked earth writing its own epitaph
and empty bowls reaching for the world's charity.

What is the colour of evil I asked of Red
who said blood speaks your language as well as mine
but take comfort from the rose
and the anonymous heart of a Valentine.

What is the colour of evil I asked of Blue
who led me through the archives of the skies
where birds of death fashioned by the hands of men
circled in the dazzling air.

What is the colour of evil I asked of Black
who guided me through galleries and museums
where the dark was equated with the beast of fear.
Then stepping through doorways of ancient lore I found darkest

chaos was a mothering force that sat upon a brood of stars.

What is the colour of evil I asked of White
who walked with me across the fugitive snow
that covered a city's scars
under an angelic apron. So I walked on in the light.

And grinned to see the pureness of a page reflecting
    my own chameleon grin.

In the Name of Country

If only you could wear
these mountains
as medals on your chest.

If only the rivers
could be impressed
with a hero's homecoming.

If only you could teach
the birds to sing
a national anthem

for one who killed
in the name of country.
Is this too much to ask?

That the trees
would salute
your steps?

That the stones
would stand
to attention?

That the grass
would wave
a small trembling flag

or at the very least
return your lost
soul?

Twins

To bring forth one
is to be blessed.

To bring forth two
is to be twice blessed.

But to bring forth
one black one white

twinned in the same womb
where day and night are one

(now here's a fine kettle
of genetic fish).

That is to enthrone
the miraculous mischief

of ovum and sperm
made flesh and bone.

That is to relearn
the lesson of the Ark –

raven and dove released
from love's tremulous flood.

Warning All Ascetics

There are devils
in the lentils.

Lucifer's Obituary to Judas

The rope has left its radiant halo
around the neck of Judas.
Was it a juniper or a cedar alas
    that suspended his body's sad tarot
for the vultures to make their chariot?
O juniper that gave foundation
    to the temple of Solomon
O cedar fragrant as the limbs of Lebanon
    What final branch of refuge for this lost son
whose intentions were less precise
    than thirty pieces of silver?
Which dove of solace will perch upon those eyes?
For your garments, dear Iscariot,
    Who will cast a solitary lot
Or balm your limbs in fabled spices?
Yet, for while, you walked the straight and narrow
    and gloried in Nazareth's numinous glow
till you stumbled against temptation.

Little did you know it was all divinely planned.
Brother, sleep well, let me be first to kiss your hand

Go On Pandora

What's a box for
if not to be opened?
What's temptation for
if no one succumbs?
A box becomes news
when someone like you
looks inside for clues
to the universe.
Call it a blessing.
Call it a curse.
No more guessing.
Go on Pandora
my enquiring daughter.
Remove the lid
of your curious Grail.
Hope will not fail.

Ride On Lady G

What's the good of riding
in naked glory
through the streets of a town
if you can't catch
the public eye?
No crowd standing by
to urge you on, sister.
No photographer
from the local press
to record your protest.
Not even a snap
for the family album
so your grandchildren
can see Gran's bum
beside a horse's.
Unless, of course,
one breaks the promise
of barred doors
and drawn curtains.
That's where I come in.
Know what I mean Lady G?
Peep he will peep he won't.
Temptation says try.
And so a tailor's eye
is immortalised
and your posterior rides
in the face of posterity.

Lucifer's Canticle for Gethsemane

I

In the Garden of Gethsemane –
there where the olives are pressed
I will put him to his hardest test.

Three temptations I have given
and thrice the man hath shamed me
by resisting every one.

Refusing to turn stones to bread
or make a flying leap of faith.
This fisher of men would not bite the bait.

Not for all the kingdom's glory
would he fall down and worship me
Get thee hence Satan for it is written

But if I am ridded of so easily
how would Eden's apple be bitten
or Gethsemane become a chapter in his story

As well as mine.

II

Tonight in Gethsemane
let uncertainty
be his halo.

Let him kneel
at the crossroads
of yes and no.

Let his mission
find uneven keel
in the anguished waters of doubt.

Let indecision
be his demon
and in his heart fear blossom.

Let him call upon
his heavenly father
to take away the cup

of ordained suffering.
Let a moment's wavering
weaken his resolve.

In a moonlit olive grove
let the juice of this man's love
be accounted for in blood.

III

And when his heart was exceeding sorrowful
Who would tarry with him but one hour? One.
Not Peter. Not James. Not John.
'Couldest not thou watch one hour?'

And I who had fallen from the grace of his eye
Watch each bleeding second furrow his face.
Innocence soon to be ensnared with a kiss.
The sheep scattered. The shepherd smitten.

No doubt he'd say 'for it is written'
and follow his cross-calling to Golgotha.
Become a dove crucified upon a hill.
Very well. Let prophecy be fulfilled.

But one hour is agony to endure
even, for one born for a halo of thorns.
He whose face is balming as the oil of olive.
He who taught to befriend a foe and forgive.

All I wanted was for him to survive
as beautiful. Open to temptation. A mothers son.
I did not want the rapture of his face gone.
I did not want the bread of his body pierced.

Believe me, even this man's garments will not go unsung.

Lucifer to Icarus

Icarus even before you flew
I could have told you a thing or two.

Beware the singeing sunlight
that will unwax your flight

And ground your feathered aspiration.
Remind you that you're after all a craftsman's son

Not a god who dwells on pedestals of clouds
or hobnobs with that seraphic crowd.

A simple boy who thought the runway of the sky
was space enough for his Concorde heart

thought he'd fly into the sun's signalling eye.
Dare the evanescent tarmac of god-given air.

Darling boy, I could have told you beware
of the treacherous purity of the blinding light

yet even as you obeyed the downward call of destiny
you would not make a god of gravity.

Freedom was the name of the demon
that gave you faith and drove you on

though some would argue curiosity
or simply say too damn stubborn.

But if deafness to Father was your fatal
Sin, I relived with you the Passion of my Fall.

For I was the little voice that said you can do it.
Be tempted to defy the tyranny of the sun.

To be frank, I knew you'd never make it.
Yet how my heart felt pierced with a sword

when your lovely body drowned. O my rebel son.

A Short Romp Among Saints

I *Absolution or Ablution?*

Cleanliness, I hear you say
is next to godliness.

Are you sure?

For I have seen the saintly
haloed in their own mess –

they who venerated their sores
as faith confirmed –

crawled on all fours
and revelled in vermin –

and considered a bath
an invitation to sin.

Does this mean
that the straight and narrow path

never leads to a sauna?

Such thoughts I ponder
under the shower.

II *St Augustine*

Take a deep theological breath
before you confess, St Augustine.
I'm not talking incontinence and sin.
I'm onto the business of breaking wind,
or to put it bluntly – 'farting'.
Let's face it. There are farters and farters.
You have your tentative breeze-teaser,
and you have your full-blown olympian gale-blower.
So let's take a backward glance
at these masters of the art
of backdoor orchestration.

That Egyptian courtier for a start
whose bowels 'sang like a harp',
especially after a banquet of beans.
That English landsman of medieval means
who curry favoured the King's presence
with a fife of flatulence.
That French music hall maestro of the rude sound –
wasn't he toasted for bringing the house down
with controlled cannonades from the bum?
And what about Salvador Dalì?
Didn't he wax with long-winded spirituum
on this most unsurrealistic act,
which is supposed to scare off a demon?
It's not for me to go on ad infinitum.

But it took a saint like you, St Augustine,
to describe the deed with just the right words:
'There are those that can break wind backwards
so artfully you would think they sang.'
Come on, Gustie, confess it's the truth.
And you said it in Latin to boot.

III *St George and the Dragon*

Who will lance
the Dragon?
Who will teach
the flaming one
the dance
of death?

Who will face
its breath
with a
patriarch's
stance?

Why you, St George
And by George
I'll be damned

But there's fire coming out of your mouth!

97

IV *St Theresa of Avila*

A penny for your thoughts,
St Theresa of Avila –
I almost said of Vanilla,
knowing that sweet tooth of yours
for the divine preserve
of quince and Easter cake.
Oh, it wasn't against your Credo
to compare a Seville patio
to slabs of iced sugar. I like that.

And to wear a woollen tunic
in summer's roasting heat,
you'd be the first to agree
was a rather penitential feat.
An inquisition of the body-part.

You're a woman after my own heart.
'Preserve us from sullen saints,'
you said. I couldn't agree more.
That's why I came knocking at your door.
I didn't mean for you to faint.
For you, I'd have done anything.
Run bubble bath. Even paint
your toes or massage your skin.

What made you call me, and I quote,
'That poor wretch who cannot love'?
Somehow, you haven't got me quite sussed.
For when the holy word goosed
your swooning throat,
I thought to myself, if such rapture
be a mystical perk,
then let love do its ensnaring work
and be my wretched capture.

v *St Michael*

It's a tricky business –
this weighing of souls,
especially when demons
are doing their best to tip
the delicate balance.
But somebody's got to do it.

And who dares question the fairness
of your archangelic metrics
that leave everything to chance?
But what I'd like to know, St Michael,
which weighs more, sunrise or nightfall?
A fallen feather or petal?
How does a halo
compare with a shadow –
I mean, kilo for kilo?
How do you measure in a scale-pan
the soul of a woman and a man?

I don't envy you, St Michael.
No greengrocer would go for your job,
even for a few extra bob.

vi *St Bridget*

St Bridget
whose footsteps blessed
the shamrock's trinity –

associate
of blacksmithery and poetry.
Druid's fair daughter

baptised
by none other than the Patriarch.
Did your mammy never tell thee

that whistling
was the domain of farmers and tarts?

Yet, good lady of Kildare,
your whistling struck
a keening note in Ireland's heart,

and it came to be
that many a wanton daughter
was fondly christened Biddy.

VII *St John the Baptist and Salomé*

Come in from the wilderness
O St John the Baptist.
Just think what you've missed.
You could have settled down
with Salomé's saucy dish
in homely coupledom.
Instead, you settled for wild locust
and a sackcloth epitaph.
Never baptised your staff
in the water of her font.
All she wanted was to mount
the ladder
of your limbs.
But the only head you gave her
was on a silver platter.
By then it didn't matter.
Alas, O hairy messenger,
she could have veiled
you in seven veils
and bid you live
to tell the tale.

Battle of the Buttocks

I

Blessed are the meek.
If someone smites you
on the left buttock,
turn the other cheek.

II

Rumour has it
I have no buttocks.
Beautiful in front.
Hollow at the back.
No comment.
I'll let that pass.
Or must I expose
my golden ass?

III

Thou art Venus Kallipygos.
And upon this rock
I will build your buttock.

IV

Hotfoot
they came from far and wide
to stare upon the bot
of Venus Hottentot.

She who spent
her final days
in a chamber of glass.

Burnt on the stake
of Europe's gaze.
Guillotined by eyes.
O what have they learnt
from the last of the tribe?

V

Lay down weapons.
Bare all buttocks.
Only the slaughtered
on the bleeding sand
will not tell the tale
of this fleshly fanfare
of surrender.

Money Money Money

The filthy rich can afford
to call it filthy lucre
but of course they never do
brooding upon their nest eggs
with the coolness of a cuckoo.
Nor do they speak of 'ill-begotten gains'
or 'the root of all evil'.
And during my own stint in Eden
I never saw a fiver or a dollar bill
hanging from the tree of Good and Evil.
Sure, a fiver in a serpent's tongue
would have looked more stylish than an apple.
Now money talks, but does it hiss,
though I've heard it called the devil's dung.
Ah. The spoor that buys a fragile bliss.

Coffee in Heaven

You'll be greeted
by a nice cup of coffee
when you get to heaven
and strains of angelic harmony.

But wouldn't you be devastated
if they only serve decaffeinated
while from the percolators of hell

your soul was assaulted
by Satan's fresh espresso smell?

Istory Lesson

If it is sluttish to drop one's aitches, then Queen Elizabeth I was a slut.
ANTHONY BURGESS: *Signals in the Dark*

If dropping er aitches
turns a queen to a slut
then a slut I shall be.

So send in a gallant
to arness me royal aunches
for I'm feeling orny.

I'll even ave a commoner
if e's ardy in bed.
But touch my maid of onour,

and so elp me God
it's off to the Tower
and good riddance to is ead.

Artist's Model

Now turn from your newspaper, friend.
whether couched in art or legend
by a black hand or a white,
look for the one with head of horns
– that mastermind of human plight.
But it's time I set the record right.

Look towards the holy grotesqueries
of your cathedral gargoyles
and the margins of your breviaries
delicately drawn with devilries
as if you could marginalise
the revelries of so-called sin.
Well, take it from me, art or no art,
I'm central to the scheme of things.
The masterpiece displayed
on the canvas of the heart.
And do you know I've been portrayed
more often than my rival model: God

Without wanting to sound immodest
I've given artists little rest.
Even Goya who painted bleeding Christ
thought horns also deserved the limelight.
Not to mention Hieronymous Bosch
(H.B. to intimates like me)
whose imagery makes me say 'Gosh,
such divinity, such devilry!'
And goatish features well-hung in a gallery
seem so photogenic so contemporary.
The Muse that answers to the name of Devil
has inspired pen and brush and chisel.
I've even watched myself on video.
But my profile looks best in soft medieval glow.

Devil Diva

Tonight I'll rock
the boat.
Invite Beelzebub
to my throat.
Play havoc
with bel canto.
Screw fortissimo.

Tonight I'll let
my hormones
have the last word.
Time for the crone
to take over.
The high notes
can go to hell.

And as for them
bleeding roses –
they can stick 'em
up their arias.
And if they insist
then they can kiss
my coloraturas.

The Devil's Advice to Old Couplers

So what if his prick
can no longer raise its senile
head. Whisper something vile
into his octogenarian ear
to tinkle the glass of his spine.

So what if her bosom
has now lowered its flag.
Her mind still basks in talk of shag.
And you can at least salute
her with your shrivelled root.

Come all ye couplers.
Now the curtain is drawn
set fire to your autumnal straws.
Frolic among a haystack of wrinkles.
Seize time by the crotch.
Make the Grim Reaper blush.

Or must I repeat in those doting ears of thine
that Sara at ninety saw pregnancy signs
and Abraham at ninety-nine was circumcised?

Barbed Wire

Barbed wire, your thorns bear
no redeeming heart or rose –
only a desperate bloom
already become living shadows.

And through time's twisted telescope
I see guardian angels
in goose-stepping boots
and a Greek chorus of Greenham women
nurturing the stubborn flame
of hope.

O Cassandra, be my comforter,
feed me plums of gloom
that I may read history's hidden thoughts.

Barbed wire, another name
for you is 'Devil's Rope'.
Yet in your thorned presence
even demons are impressed

by the hand that could fashion
so silent a witness
to the choreography of the doomed.

Question Time with the Devil

When cries of heresy
followed women to the final stake
Did the Devil help to stoke the flames?

When webs of ancestry
became nameless cargo in a ship
Did the Devil chart and log the trip?

When walking elegies
were smothered in a womb of gas
Did the Devil supervise the task?

When the desert bloomed with bodies
and the mother of battles wept
Did the Devil count the score of death?

When tribal rivalry
tore the heart out of Rwanda
Did the Devil share in the plunder?

When divided loyalty
likewise made the heart of Ireland bleed
Did the Devil dance a jig and reel?

When Bosnia shed its grief
down the smooth cheeks of a TV screen
Did the Devil have a peaceful sleep?

O what would you do without me to blame?
But was it one with horns and fiendish looks
who pushed the button and wrote the history books?

I give you half a minute to reply.

Progress

The toad's jewel
has erupted into venom.

The flowering shrub
has drawn a pilgrimage of slugs.

The split atom
has blossomed into a bomb.

The glinting ore
has grown a constellation of swords.

And the cloned goat
ponders its bearded lookalike

in a blazing mirage of knowledge.

Bridge Builder

Bridge-builder I am
between the holy and the damned
between the bitter and the sweet
between the chaff and the wheat

Bridge-builder I am
between the goat and the lamb
between the sermon and the sin
between the princess and Rumpelstiltskin

Bridge-builder I am
between the yoni and the lingam
between the darkness and the light
between the left hand and the right

Bridge-builder I am
between the storm and the calm
between the nightmare and the sleeper
between the cradle and the Reaper

Bridge-builder I am
between the hex and the hexagram
between the chalice and the cauldron
between the gospel and the Gorgon

Bridge-builder I am
between the serpent and the wand
between the hunter and the hare
between the curse and the prayer

Bridge-builder I am
between the hanger and the hanged
between the water and the wine
between the pearls and the swine

Bridge-builder I am
between the beast and the human
for who can stop the dance
of eternal balance?

5

poems from
LOVELINES TO A GOAT-BORN LADY

For Grace

Circles

Mud is transformed by hopscotch circles of light.
Your little girl legs flounce free as rain.
You redesign creation in small hops.

Now let's hopscotch back into the first garden.
Let's invite the serpent to our circle.
Let's share an apple with a touch of salt.

On the Waters

Asleep, your body is a ship
bound for dreamland.
I come into bed like a stowaway.

Adrift, on the waters of contradiction
who can tell ship from water
stowaway from dreamer?

Somewhere

Somewhere in her body
there must be a hidden forest.
Somewhere in this forest
there must be a hidden bush.
Somewhere in this bush
there must be a hidden creek.
Somewhere in this creek
there must be hidden wealth.
But I have not come to speak of diamonds.
I have merely come to bathe my mouth
and taste the secret of her water.

No Ordinary Thing

Small days walk on stilts.
Mother Sally dances in your childhood eye.
Masquerade magic rivets you to a window,
eyes wide enough to accommodate a ritual,
and what the drum doing to you
will not be mentioned in your passport.

Small days get high on fruit.
Your young mouth dismembers a starapple
that stains lips with innocent semen.
I conjure you, little red girl
back in a tropical time,
willing your own nipples into bud.
Rudeness is part of your heritage.
Your mother, playing the piano,
scolds you for repeating a brazen folksong.
You discover geography between your legs
but go to bed with Enid Blyton.

Now wrap a warm scarf around your neck
and think of the tropical riddles that reside
beneath your winter coat.

No ordinary thing, my love.

Lovepoem Slowly Turning into a Lullaby

Starapple of my eye
my firefly in pitchdense of night.
Sleep tight on the drift of your dreams.
This is a lovepoem slowly turning into a lullaby

My salt and pepper
when ole higue shedding sly skin,
my wide sheet over mirror
when lightning scrawling sky.
Sleep tight on the drift of your dreams.
This is a lovepoem slowly turning into a lullaby.

Lucky seed in my palm of hope,
my heavensent in hard guava season.
Sleep tight on the drift of your dreams.
This is a lovepoem slowly turning into a lullaby.

My white rum whisperings
from the corner of my heart,
my good breeze tidings
to so many unanswerable whys.
Sleep tight on the drift of your dreams.
This is a lovepoem slowly turning into a lullaby.

By All Means Bless

By all means
bless the cloth
that wiped
the face
of Jesus

By all means
bless the towel
that unfolds
an infant
like miraculous bread

By all means
bless the towel
the boxer returns to
– a brief harbour
after a harassing round

By all means
bless the sacred silk
that garbs
the sumo's
amplitude of loin

But I say this also
bless the towel
that unwraps
your buttocks
(fresh out of the shower)
with such casual ease

we overlook
life's small epiphanies

Moonbelly

1

Your belly can no longer be anonymous
even in full-blown blouse.
Pregnancy is now your landscape
and fullness comes to claim your shape.

2

Drumseed
        a-bloom
wit de speed
        of water

daddywater
        meet
mammywater
        in one twinkling

monthly blood
turn back
it own tide

monthly blood
have new mouth
to feed

an new mouth is new bud

When mammywater
an daddywater
meet

Wit god blessing
spirits willing

        navel string
            soon sing

3

It is a globe –
your belly big with child.
Granted you cannot spin it
to trace a country with a finger,
but it is a globe.

On its still axis
unmapped waters turn
a world coming into view
by loving degrees.
A continent is happening.

Your belly big with child
is geography made new,
and your navel the centre
from which all marvels
take their bearings.

4

Moonbelly
moonbelly
mind how yu go

moonbelly
moonbelly
take it slow

moonbelly
moonbelly
go carefully
among the hurrying crowds

remember
elbows have edges
and pointed umbrellas
think they own the world

moonbelly
moonbelly
mind how yu go

moonbelly
moonbelly
take it slow

5

I will miss
that brown moon
rising over your pubic crest
eclipsing your knickers' horizon

When your belly reclaims its flatness,
I will miss watching you stand
in the bloom of your own reflection.

7

poems from

HALF-CASTE
&
WE BRITS

From Britannia To Whom It May Concern

Thank you for the kind thought, the compliment
of once calling me mother country.
You make an island feel like a continent.

When I ruled the waves, all the world seemed pink.
I manipulated maps with sword and cross.
Shifted boundaries with seal of royal ink.

I enthroned my language as a rule of tongue.
Gathered India's jewels into my crown.
And Africa's blood still haunts my monuments.

How can I turn from history's looking-glass
when even my sugar holds a bitter past?
The sea has been my girdle and my guilt.

Though darkness enriches my red white and blue,
I've learnt how the sun sets on empires.
And the voiceless voice their righteous fires.

Now, old ruptures bless me with hybrid webs.
I feel horizons throbbing at my doorstep.
My streets pulse with a plurality of tongues.

And mother country has much work to do.
I must prepare my cliffs for new homecomings.
Tie yellow ribbons round my children's minds.

Half-caste

Excuse me
standing on one leg
I'm half-caste

Explain yuself
wha yu mean
when yu say half-caste
yu mean when picasso
mix red an green
is a half-caste canvas/
explain yuself
wha yu mean
when yu say half-caste
yu mean when light an shadow
mix in de sky
is a half-caste weather/
well in dat case
england weather
nearly always half-caste
in fact some o dem cloud
half-caste till dem overcast
so spiteful dem dont want de sun pass
ah rass/
explain yuself
wha yu mean
when yu say half-caste
yu mean when tchaikovsky
sit down at dah piano
an mix a black key
wid a white key
is a half-caste symphony/

Explain yuself
wha yu mean
Ah listening to yu wid de keen
half of mih ear
Ah lookin at yu wid de keen
half of mih eye
an when I'm introduced to you
I'm sure you'll understand
why I offer yu half-a-hand
an when I sleep at night

I close half-a-eye
consequently when I dream
I dream half-a-dream
an when moon begin to glow
I half-caste human being
cast half-a-shadow
but yu must come back tomorrow

wid de whole of yu eye
an de whole of yu ear
an de whole of yu mind

an I will tell yu
de other half
of my story

Ignatius Sancho Returns The Compliment

A white fellow once said in praise of me:
'God's image, though cut in ebony.'
And I, a dark fellow, said of him kindly:
'God's image, though cut in ivory.'

Oh! The pleasures of novelty to youth! – we went by water –
had a coach home – were gazed at – followed &c. &c. –
but not much abused.
– The Letters of Ignatius Sancho, 27 August 1777

Caribbean Eye Over Yorkshire

(for John Lyons)

Eye
perched over
adopted Yorkshire.

Eye christened
in Caribbean blue
and Trinidad sunfire.

Eye tuned in
to the flame
tree's decibels

and the red
stereophonic bloom of immortelles.

Eye once a stranger
to silver birch and conifer
now on first-name terms

with beech and elm and alder.
Eye making an ally
of heather and lavender.

Eye of painter
eye of poet
eye of prankster

eye looking into linden
for ghost-traces
of silk-cotton

eye of crow
in carnival cape
seeing inward

eye of blackbird
casting
humming-bird shadow.

Coconuts' Reply

We whose insides
you brand as white
though our outsides
are wholemeal brown.

Not black enough
in talk and stride.
Too Englishified
in style and tongue.

We Coconuts
who you say talk posh.
Yuppie devotees
of a god called Dosh.

We wear no crown
of bold blackness
or flaunt with ease
our roots on our sleeves.

Like the coconut
that versatile fruit
you named us after.
We too spill water.

Crack our brown shells.
Probe our white pith.
See for yourself
how horizons sit.

Africa's fountain
waiting to be spilt
from Europe's veins.
We Coconuts.

Taking the Dogma for a Walk

Whatever its colour or its breed –
it's wise to keep your dogma on a lead
for many a dogma has been known
to settle for a human bone.

A dogma can turn on its owner.
A bit like what's called friendly fire.
A dogma can bite the hand that feeds it,
however much you shout *Sit! Sit!*

Dogmas tend to sniff other dogmas.
Then dogma joins dogma in heat.
This can happen on your own sofa
or in front of an entire street.

People, they say, begin to resemble
the dogma they keep for companion.
I watch my dogma's physiognomy
for traces of my own expression.

But it's not as easy as it sounds.
A dogma is good at disguising its mug.
Now a do-gooder, now a thug.
Both wagging with toothsome conviction.

Union Jack and Union Jill

Union Jack
and Union Jill
went up the hill
for a patriotic fling.

One waved a flag
and marched up and down.
One sang an anthem
and saluted after.

But they stole a quick kiss
as they talked politics
and soon love grew taller
than their raised fists.

For Union Jack
and Union Jill
the grass stood still
the hill hoisted its bliss.

And they rolled over
in a peal of laughter
to find their convictions
all flying in tatters.

'Love Calls Us Back from Simplification'

*(For Eavan Boland, who made this comment during a poetry
reading at the Voice Box, Royal Festival Hall, April 1992.)*

Out of the mouth of an Irish woman
pebbles of love play ducks and drakes
across the April face of the river Thames.

Tonight the voice will not be boxed-in
by man-made dimensions or canons of sin,
The tongue revelling in connection.

Let griot seaniche tinker obeahwoman
raise a glass to the health of contradiction.
Now Carrickfergus merge with Caribbean.

Love calls us back from simplification.

To reduce a nation to a label
To reduce a race to an assumption
To reduce a face to a formula of black and white.

To hang a stereotype around the heart
To build a wall with stones of conviction
To let the map dictate affection.

To allow boundaries their frozen dance
To grant frontiers their fixity of expression
To make a monument of an ism.

But love calls us back from simplification.
Tonight in a room above a river above a city
a poet is sharing the bread of her words

and we walking out blessed with resonance.

Boomerang

Featherless bird
I will nest in the eye of wind

Crescent moon
fashioned by hand
I will slice the sky of your gaze

Crooked stick
I will aspire to the gift of wings

Rainbow wood
I will bridge what is and is not imagined
forever curving towards the path of origin

Hurl me from your hand. But
remember.
I am the dream the wind has
given you.

A Vampire's Priorities

Today I want to do green things.
Eavesdrop on the gossip of leaves.
Tune in to the voices of trees.
Translate every whisper of grass.
Put myself in the place of spring.
Even something as simple
as eat a granny smith apple.
Today I want to do green things.

But there are red things to be done.
A rose to savour.
A flame to tend to.
Another throat to treasure.

The Hurt Boy and the Birds

The hurt boy talked to the birds
and fed them the crumbs of his heart.

It was not easy to find the words
for secrets he hid under his skin.
The hurt boy spoke of a bully's fist
that made his face a bruised moon –
his spectacles stamped to ruin.

It was not easy to find the words
for things that nightly hissed
as if his pillow was a hideaway for creepy-crawlies –
the note sent to the girl he fancied
held high in mockery.

But the hurt boy talked to the birds
and their feathers gave him welcome –

Their wings taught him new ways to become.

On a Yazoo Stem

(for Michael Horovitz)

Bespectacled hopper
for all rhymes and seasons.
Squirrel bopper
gathering nutty poems
from Albion's unsung corners.

Runaway sunflower
climbing Blake's staircase
on a yazoo stem
grown-up still at play
with creepy-crawly friends.

I have seen you in rush-hour haste
rucksackladen yet open to embrace
bearing that vulnerable aura
that mocks a mugger's fists.

Torch-bearer schemer
of poetry olympics
not beyond elfish tricks
when the canon aims its metronome.

But beyond the halo of eccentrics
and the zany loom you weave
the hasidic child is at home
under your colourful shirt

remembering holocausts
at nations' doorsteps
yet taking hope
in a hosanna of bay leaves.

Marriage of Opposites

I Copper,
child of Fire,
married Zinc,
child of Water,
and gave birth
to a daughter
called Brass.

I Copper,
child of the Sun,
married Tin,
child of the Moon,
and gave birth
to a son
called Bronze.

I Copper,
proud parent
of peaceful bell
and flaming sword,
have many
a story
to tell.

Windrush Child

(for Vince Reid, the youngest passenger
on the Empire Windrush, *then aged 13)*

Behind you
Windrush child
palm trees wave goodbye

above you
Windrush child
seabirds asking why

around you
Windrush child
blue water rolling by

beside you
Windrush child
your Windrush mum and dad

think of storytime yard
and mango mornings

and new beginnings
doors closing and opening

will things turn out right?
At least the ship will arrive
in midsummer light

and you Windrush child
think of grandmother
telling you don't forget to write

and with one last hug
walk good walk good
and the sea's wheel carries on spinning

and from that place England
you tell her in a letter
of your Windrush adventure

stepping in a big ship
not knowing how long the journey
or that you're stepping into history

bringing your Caribbean eye
to another horizon
grandmother's words your shining beacon

learning how to fly
the kite of your dreams
in an English sky

Windrush child
walking good walking good
in a mind-opening
meeting of snow and sun

Salt

Once used as Roman currency,
now a common guest at your table.
Sprinkle me over your food and your soul.
I'm known to preserve as well as corrode.
A pinch of me tests the grain of truth.
So spill me if you dare to tempt fate.
In the hands of a Sumo wrestler,
I'm a shower of invocation.
No need to rub me into your wounds.
I'm at home in your sweat and your tears.
Fine or coarse, I can teach you to melt
into the miracle of yourself.

Coal

My body heaved to the hacking of picks.
Fuelled your industry and politics.
I warmed your houses, I stoked your hearth.
Fed you my black carbonaceous heart.
My forsaken pits still send a bitter chill.
Or have you forgotten names like Scargill?
My slumbering slagheaps stalk your history
like the death-song of a canary.
I am the smouldering lump that speaks volumes,
the dark ember glowing in a white room,
a nugget of lost solidarity.

Testing Time

(in memory of Ted Hughes)

October's end
has gathered more than fallen leaves
for earth's keeping

The seasons
open their door to the voice
that spoke for them

November moon
comes to harvest one who rejoiced
in its shadow

Rivers reclaim
one they consider laureate
of their blood's flow

Grasses play God
and welcome you who listened
to their requiem

Sky's granary
regains the wheat of your word-hoard's
unwritten poems

The howling wolf
gives back your name to the wind
that lent you breath

Prometheus grins
because you have returned the loan
of that fire

The fox weeps
when cunning acknowledges grief
as superior

The salmon leaps
under veils of water for this
is how they mourn

In roe-deer's eye
there is condolence and prayer
expressed as one

Thrushes lend
their choir to the hymnal air
for you their scribe

The sheep prepare
bundles of comfort for they've heard
of your coming

Over Crow Hill
nightfall embraces your black songs
as is fitting

And it is right
that oak and elm kneel in vigil
at your passing

For they stand firm
in the soil of your syllables
testing time.

Three in the Snow

(for Gillian Clarke and James Berry)

1

Cars are iced cakes
on four wheels going nowhere

trees put on their mantillas
of icicles

roofs become sloping rinks
with no hope of daredevil skate

roads turn candyfloss lakes
for dazzling jaws of headlights

phoneboxes are frosty cubicles
where your last coin

is held tenderly
as your first fire.

2

In a deluge of snowfall
whiteness pirouettes
on numbing tiptoe
and a rainbow
is an extinct creature
in this February freeze.
Even the smallest country road
aspires to the Alps.

This is weather
for sensible wellies
not ankle-low shoes.
Thank God for Gillian's boots
(which I borrow)
Survivors of Welsh valleys
granting sanctuary
to a pair of West Indian feet.

Or shall I say a pair of ravens
in a homely ark
making their covenant
with the snow-white dark?

3

This is not the humming-bird hour
when nectar secrets are revealed
and gods come disguised in tiny feathers.

No palm tree outside a window
to display a familiar majesty
as far as hungry eye can see.

Here instead a birch, a yew, an elm,
an oak maybe (I couldn't say which).
And a blackbird sits on Sylvia Plath's tree.

This is not the place where the hibiscus
dares you look inside its brazen bloom.
This is Hebden Bridge where snowbound slopes defy taxi.

And so we walk to the main road, Gillian, James and me
(thank you, brother, for the marmalade on toast and tea)
– three figures warmly wrapped in talk.

Together we walk, Jamaica, Wales, Guyana, we motley three
planting in snow our footsteps' anonymous flags.

A Hand on a Forehead
(after a photograph by Sebastião Salgado)

You don't have to be a refugee on a bus
from Zepa to Zenica
to understand that in the grammar of grief,
loss is not a noun
but an eternal verb.
And when words desert us,
the doing of a hand on a forehead,
besieged by memory,
bears witness to all frontlines
crosses all frontiers
speaks all mother tongues.
When the brain becomes a battleground,
and the past insists
on being the present tense,
a hand on a forehead needs no translator.

Dr Johnson, a Jamaican and a Dictionary (1755)

A harmless drudge, a lexicographer.
What shall I do without Francis Barber,
my Jamaican-born companion,
less a servant than an adopted son?
Yet the signs in those transatlantic eyes
tell me that he won't be patronised.
How vile to me is that word slavery
which I must define for my dictionary,
binding conscience to concise definition.
And what would this dull labour of language
mean to ones still born in voiceless bondage?
Ah well, Francis, pour me another one.
Let us drink to the next insurrection
when words unsettle iron's tyranny.

Dialogue

Out of a scattering of tongues
out of Babel's inheritance

How reassemble sense
from this gift of rich confusion?

How resurrect a rainbow
from a tower of ruins?

How begin to begin
the dance of utterance?

So armed with my hybrid dictionary
– a not so concise Oxford –

I face the wilderness of the Word,
letting English be my bridge

to a world harvest –
a gathering from continents

retracing empire's footsteps
seeking this time not global glory

but dialogue in the distance.

Tongue

Small flame
under the roof
of a mouth.
You devour
You cleanse
You tell honey
from vinegar.
You speak truth.
You speak slander.
You soothe
with a kiss.
You bruise
with a word.

To the possessed
you are the gift
of enlightenment.
To the dispossessed
you are the scale
of judgement.

Small flame
under the roof
of a mouth.

Tyranny knows
your hiding place.

8

selected

POEMS FOR YOUNGER READERS

Ask Mummy Ask Daddy

When I ask Daddy
Daddy says ask Mummy

When I ask Mummy
Mummy says ask Daddy.
I don't know where to go.

Better ask my teddy.
He never says no.

Don't Call Alligator Long Mouth Till You Cross River

Call alligator long-mouth
call alligator saw-mouth
call alligator pushy-mouth
call alligator scissors-mouth
call alligator raggedy-mouth
call alligator bumpy-bum
call alligator all dem rude word
but better wait
till you cross river

First Morning

I was there on that first morning of creation
when heaven and earth occupied one space
and no one had heard of the human race.

I was there on that first morning of creation
when a river rushed from the belly of an egg
and a mountain rose from a golden yolk.

I was there on that first morning of creation
when the waters parted like magic cloth
and the birds shook feathers at the first joke.

Prayer to Laughter

O Laughter
giver of relaxed mouths

you who rule our belly with tickles
you who come when not called
you who can embarrass us at times

send us stitches in our sides
shake us till the water reaches our eyes
buckle our knees till we cannot stand

we whose faces are grim and shattered
we whose hearts are no longer hearty
O Laughter we beg you

crack us up
crack us up

Egg-and-Spoon Race

One school sports day,
in the egg-and-spoon race,
        the egg ran away
        from the spoon.

The egg brought first place
but the judges said: 'Let's disqualify
the egg.
It should have waited on the spoon.'

The egg said: 'Why not disqualify
the spoon
for not catching up with me?
I'll never understand the mystery

        of the human race.'

The Speller's Bag

Here a bone.
Here a stone.
In my bag
I keep them all.

A stone brought me
by the sea.
A bone taken from where
I'll never tell thee.

A bone, a stone,
a feather, a shell,
all in my bag
to cast a spell.

A shell that taught
the wind to howl.
A feather stolen
from the back of an owl.

Then again it might be
from a raven's neck.
I'll never tell thee.

Look inside all who dare.

Inside my bag
you'll find your fear.

Fisherman Chant

Sister river
Brother river
Mother river
Father river
O life giver
O life taker
O friend river
What have you
in store
for a poor
fisherman
today?

From my boat
I cast my net
to your heart
O friend river
and I hope
you return it
gleaming with silver
O friend river

Sister river
Brother river
Mother river
Father river
O life giver
O life taker
O friend river
What have you
in store
for a poor
fisherman
today?

Rat Race

Rat race?
Don't make us laugh.
It's you humans
who're always in a haste.

Ever seen a rat
in a bowler hat
rushing to catch a train?

Ever seen a rat
with a briefcase
hurrying through the rain?

And isn't it a fact
that all that hurry-hurry
gives you humans heart attacks?

No, my friend,
we rats relax.

Pass the cheese,
please.

Hippo Writes a Love Poem to His Wife

Oh my beautiful fat wife
Larger to me than life
Smile broader than the river Nile
My winsome waddlesome
You do me proud in the shallow of morning
You do me proud in the deep of night
Oh, my bodysome mud-basking companion.

Hippo Writes a Love Poem to Her Husband

Oh my lubby-dubby hubby-hippo
With your widely-winning lippo
My Sumo-thrasher of water
Dearer to me than any two-legger
How can I live without
Your ponderful potamus pout?

Swimming Teeth

I'm not a do-as-you're-told fish.
A looked-at-in-a-bowl fish.
A stay-still-to-behold fish.
An as-you-can-guess goldfish.

Where sea is blue, I make it red.
Where body bubbles, I slash, I shred.
Where eyes see light, I blur them dark.
Where skin shines bright, I expose a heart.

Humans call me shark.
But to my friends of the deep
I am known as SWIMMING TEETH.
And one day I'd like to direct a movie.

Crocodile's Tale

The last man who mistook me for a log
Lost half-a-foot and can no longer jog.

Bedbugs Marching Song

Bedbugs
Have the right
To bite.

Bedbugs
Of the world
Unite.

Don't let
These humans
Sleep too tight.

The Hands of Trees

The hands of trees
reaching for air.
The hands of trees
clasped in a prayer.

The hands of trees
say welcome birds.
The hands of trees –
no need for words.

The Circle and the Square

Said the circle
to the square:
it appears
your corners
are all the same.
I've counted four
and bet you can't roll
as I can do
when I'm a ball.

Said the square
to the circle:
Good luck to you,
but isn't it the truth
that a ball must bear
the kicks of a boot?
So you roll wherever you go
I'll stay right here
and be a window.

Said the circle
to the square:
O what a pity
you can't come with me
when I rise to the air
as a nice bright bubble.
And wait till you see
the full-moon I can be,
the best of round and yellow.

Said the square
to the circle:
Bubbles burst, as you know,
and many a night,
the moon doesn't show.
I'm happy, thank you,
to be a window.
I enjoy the view.
I am my own little sky.
I am the house's eye.

Anyone for Pi?

Pie in the sky.
Pie in the face.
Both bring a smile
to the human race.

But the pie that fills
with most wonder of all
is the pie they serve
at the mathematicians' ball

for their *pi* has no *e*
– it's no ordinary pastry –
and they sit in circles
of opulence

as they feast on diameter
and circumference.

'It's the ratio that matters,'
they conclude with a sigh
as they raise their glasses to *pi*.
'Come hell, come heaven,
let's propose a toast
to twenty-two over seven.'

Hello H₂O

Your body
is an ocean's body,
your skin
is a river's skin.

In your footsteps
the rain dances,
in your shadow
a lake sees itself.

With your echo
a waterfall speaks,
with your gestures
a fountain splashes itself.

You leave your singature
in puddles and leaks
– each a small reminder
that water was here.

Hello H_2O,
my two parts hydrogen,
one part oxygen friend
from my womb-swimming past.

My mouth will always be your glass.

Who'll Save Dying Man?

Who'll save dying Man?
   I, said the Baboon.
Transplant my bone marrow,
and he'll wake tomorrow.

Who'll save dying Man?
   I, said the Chimpanzee
He's welcome to my brain,
for deep down we're the same.

Who'll save dying Man?
   I, said the Pig.
I'll give him my liver.
May he live forever.

Who'll save dying Man?
   I, said the Sheep.
Let him have my kidney
and that would be for free.

Who'll save dying Man?
   I, said the Rat.
My retina would do
to make his vision new.

Who'll save dying Man?
   I, said the Squid.
He can have our nerve cells,
for sea-folk wish him well.

Who'll save dying Man?
   I, said the Physician.
I'll save him with my skills,
though dying Man once killed.

Thanks for the offer,
   said dying Man.
But I'd like to request
a Dodo for a doner.

And the animals fell
a-whispering secretly:
   O dying Man
has lost his memory.

DVD RUNNING ORDER

**   *not included in the book*
†   *with Keith Waithe*